BREAKING CYCLES

A Story of Breaking Cycles of Abuse

Jenarda Makupson

Copyright © 2022 by Jenarda Makupson

All rights reserved. No portion of this book may be reproduced in any form without permission from the publisher, except as permitted by US copyright law

Contents

INTRODUCTION 1

CHAPTER 1: CHILDHOOD FULL OF DREAMS 7

CHAPTER 2: SHATTERED DREAMS 14

CHAPTER 3: PIVOTAL MOMENTS 20

CHAPTER 4: IGNORING THE RED FLAGS 26

CHAPTER 5: TYPES OF ABUSE & IPV (INTIMATE PARTNER VIOLENCE) ... 41

CHAPTER 6: ALWAYS FIGHTING FOR MY LIFE 54

CHAPTER 7: I'M GOING BACK TO CALI 69

CHAPTER 8: GUT INSTINCT 74

CHAPTER 9: FEAR OF THE UNKNOWN 83

CHAPTER 10: FORGIVING AND MOVING FORWARD 96

DEDICATION- 100

INTRODUCTION

This is not a Cinderella story. Definitely not a fairy tale. Not even that good of an after-school special to be honest with you. It's my story and it has a lot of rough edges, broken dreams, and broken promises. My childhood was full of joy, my mother did her very best to keep a smile on my face. She made sure that her kids were in extracurricular activities such as acting, dance, and modeling. As a young mother I feel that my mom did the best that she knew how to do under the circumstances, as a very young mother of two children by the time she was nineteen, although, I feel that my mom did her best it still was a lot of heartache to come as I started to approached my teenage years, and the first part of my adult life was even more traumatizing... I found out early in life that living the life of luxury, nice clothes, nice cars, and a nice home didn't mean a thing when you didn't have someone who treated you right. Someone who loves and cares about you, but rather sees you as an object with no feelings. Like a trophy to show off when they want, and toss you to the side when they are done. Like an object without feelings.

Seen objectively from a long way down the road, I know that my struggles in life come in cycles. There's a pattern here, and it's not a pleasant one to think about or reflect back on. But it is important, not only for my own peace of mind but as a warning and a lesson for young women all around the world. If I can help even one woman avoid the sort of trap I kept falling into, I will feel like this entire life I've lived has been worth it.

My history with abuse started when I was a teenager and continued on into my adult life, especially after I became married. The experience of mental, physical, financial and sexual abuse and it got worse as the years went on. I know there are many of you who will read this story and wonder to yourselves, "Why didn't she just get out?" It's a question I asked myself every single day, until I soul searched. There were so many times in my failed marriage where every single instinct was telling me to run, to hide, to go to the police, to tell a relative or a friend or a member of my congregation what was going on and ask for help. The worst part of that is that I know there are so many good people out there who would have risen to the occasion and had my back, if I would have kept trying.

I tried to leave a few times; he would always catch me at the door with my bags packed. Yes, he even had cameras in the house and I gave up on trying to escape. Why? There are a lot of reasons I can tell you, but I think the one that keeps coming up over and over again is that I was afraid. Afraid of what might be on the other side of that equation. Afraid of what it might look like to be alone and have to financially provide for my children without their father. Afraid of getting a divorce and being separated from my children. Afraid of what my ex-husband might do to me if I told him I didn't want to be with him anymore. Afraid that no one else would ever want me because I was a young mother with children and I would look as damaged on the outside as I felt on the inside which is what he always made sure to remind me of. He always would remind me that nobody would want me except for him. That is one of the lines that a man uses when he wants to emotionally abuse you and scar you, he wants you to feel like you are worthless. Which is far from true.

As I slowly came to realize however, any life is better than the one where someone else abuses you physically, mentally, emotionally, financially and sexually. That is no kind of life at all. That's an existence where you convince yourself that things will be OK and improve if you're just patient and caring and understanding and you act perfectly and don't do the kind of things that are going to upset that other person in your relationship. Over time you stop seeing them as a partner and someone who loves you and start viewing them as a kind of ticking time bomb that is apt to go off at the slightest provocation. Eventually, you're walking on pins and needles around them. Yes, that is what I said, I felt as if I was walking on pins and needles all the time, in my own home! Now you tell me if that is a way for a young woman to live? When they're happy, you'll do anything in the world to keep them happy. When they're upset or sad or angry, you're just praying that their outburst won't be too bad or that if it is, the kids won't see it or hear it. Thinking in those terms, in retrospect, filled me with shame and guilt for the situation I let my kids and myself fester in for so many years. It was a fake life and unfortunately the kind of life that far too many other women let themselves fall into without knowing how to escape.

Before I start my story, I want to give you some statistics on domestic abuse that I hope will help you understand that you are not alone, that your situation is not unique, and that the only way to heal a relationship where one person raises their hands in anger against another is to get out of it.

- ☞ 1 in 4 women experience severe intimate partner physical violence, intimate partner contacts sexual violence, and/or intimate partner stalking with impacts such as injury, fearfulness, post-traumatic stress disorder (PTTS0, use of victim services, or contraction of sexually-transmitted diseases in their lifetimes.

- ☞ On average, nearly 20 people per minute are physically abused by an intimate partner in the United States. That equates to more than 10 million people in an entire year.

- ☞ 1 in 3 women have experienced some form of physical violence from an intimate partner, such as slapping, shoving, pushing, kicking, or hitting.

- ☞ 1 in 4 women have been victims of severe physical violence such as beating, strangling, or burning, by an intimate partner in their lifetime.

- ☞ 1 in 7 women have been stalked by an intimate partner to the point that they felt very fearful or believed that they or someone close to them would either be harmed or killed.

- ☞ Women between 18 years old and 24 years old are most commonly abused by an intimate partner.

☞ 1 in 5 women have been raped in their lifetimes.

☞ Of those, 45.4% of female rape victims were raped by an intimate partner.

☞ 1 in 15 children is exposed to intimate partner violence each year, and 90% of these children are eyewitnesses to the violence.

☞ Victims of intimate partner violence lose a total of 8 million days of paid work each year.

☞ Between 2003 and 2008, 142 women were murdered in their workplace by their abuser. This figure accounted for 78% of all women killed in the workplace in that time frame.

☞ 72% of all murder-suicides involve an intimate partner. 94% of the victims in these murder-suicides are female.

Statistics furnished by the National Council Against Domestic Violence

So what happened to me? Where did this precocious, happy, go-lucky child make the wrong turns and wind up having to fight for her life before she finally broke free? To understand it all, you have to start at the beginning. So that's just what we'll do.

CHAPTER 1

CHILDHOOD FULL OF DREAMS

I was born in Cleveland, Ohio in the 1970's. Cleveland wasn't the best place for African-Americans at that time. There had been calls against housing discrimination and redlining to keep blacks out of traditionally white neighborhoods. My parents were high school sweethearts. My parents dated on and off since they were fourteen years old. My mother and father were a nice-looking young couple. Mom was light skinned, petite curvy, with pretty black shiny hair and my father had smooth brown skin, with a splash of red, something like an Indian, his hair was black and curly, his teeth straight and white, all the ladies loved him. He had a smooth low deep tone to his voice, not only is my father handsome he is very smart, his goal before getting drafted to war was to be a doctor. My dad had been in the Army and when he was enrolled, he had been exposed to and became addicted to drugs, like a lot of our soldiers. When his service time ended, he kept on using drugs that flooded into the urban and low-income areas and medical school was sadly forgotten for the time being. My mom didn't want us living in that environment anymore - a city on the decline and with her and my father using drugs. My mom said that she just looked around one day and did not want that life for her children anymore, so she got a divorce from my father when I was just a new baby in the late 70's and moved us with her out to the golden shores of sunny Southern California.

One of my mom's cousins was already living in California and living what we called the "Hollywood life", working at Motown Records. Motown might have started in Detroit, but it had moved to Los Angeles after the riots of the late 1960s. The biggest acts in the business were churning out hits from Motown - The Temptations, Marvin Gaye, Gladys Knight & The Pips, Stevie Wonder, and Diana Ross, just to name a few.

My mom followed her cousin's lead and got a job working for Motown Records and Venture Records. It was a great thing for her and she was able to shine and get out there and meet people. She was still incredibly young and beautiful, she would always get attention from men when she came up to my school, none of the children, teachers and parents even believed that she was our mom because she looked so young. She was torn between enjoying her life, and taking care of her children. She worked so much that my sister and I were staying at home by ourselves at a very young age. My sister was always so pretty to me. She had straight long black hair, pretty smooth brown skin, pretty brown eyes with extremely long eyelashes, her eyelashes were so long that you could barely see her eyes. My big sister helped watch me and take care of me. We were cooking dinner so it would be on the table when my mom came home from work and we were staying home by ourselves. We knew to call my mom at work and ask her if we could go outside and play after we did our chores. We were very responsible at a very young age, and always came in before the streetlights came on. It wasn't the best life but it was better than a lot of people I knew. Back then I really thought it was fun. My mother would say that I was like her conscience because I always would watch her and never wanted her to do anything wrong.

I remember one night after work my mom came home to our little cozy home in West L.A and she was searching everywhere for her cigarettes, I looked at her with my chubby cheeks, chubby little stomach, smooth brown skin and frizzy ponytails, just looking at her search, and then I said in my little squeaky voice, "mommy cigarettes are bad for you so I flushed them down the toilet, I don't want you to die mommy. "I was around six years old, I was always a little different and unique type of child, I was very observant and caring, I cared about animals, insects, people, I always felt like I was different, so my mom smoking was definitely not what I wanted. I remember how hard my mom would work to get me and my sister bikes, toys and clothes, somehow, she always came through.

My mom was a single mom who hung around four fly girls and I thought they were the prettiest ever, and as they say today, "baddest chics" around. All of them were young, pretty and had good jobs in the music industry. The only one of them with children was my mother. So, I am sure you can imagine how two pretty little girls were treated and spoiled rotten. One of the four fly girls who was my favorite, Carey, she was from Detroit Michigan and she had a limousine, so me and my sister would get driven to school in a limousine and all of the kids thought we were rich. We ate at the best restaurants in Malibu, Santa Monica and Beverly Hills. My mom would drop us off on some days to Modeling, Dance and acting class, it was downstairs from the record company that she was working at. I loved going, and my mom said I was a natural born star.

I remember a scout came in looking for talent and they interviewed everyone for a McDonald's commercial including me. Well, I was chosen for the commercial. I was waiting by the phone for the call to announce who was chosen, I remember getting that call, I was so excited, life was great. It was just the three of us, my sister Cheri, my mom Lauren and myself Kim. Living in Los Angeles was so fun. I lived in a single parent home for most of my life.

Thinking back when I was in kindergarten I would hang out with my friends in Los Angeles until the street lights would come on. I always was a happy go lucky child who laughed a lot and loved a lot. I remember playing double-dutch outside with my friends and walking to the corner store to get Now & Laters. If you grew up in the cool 80's I am sure that you know about Chick o-Stix, Now & Later candy and Sunflower Seeds. As I look back on growing up in California and I picture my life, I smile because I see myself with my two pony tails, chubby stomach, smooth brown skin and chunky cheeks. I can picture the sun shining on my face as I walk down the street to go to my friend's house next door to play. I remember how clean the air smelled, the warm breeze. Little things that I looked forward to in the morning, like going to my friend's house on the way to school, knocking on her door, so that her and her brother could let me in to eat donuts and milk before school in the morning. The word simplicity means so much to me now. Little things in life that mold you and make you into who you are today.

I know that I was different, a bit unique, and strange as a child because I cared about things and people so much. I always was in touch with my feelings as a child. I was the type of child that after getting spanked, would still want a hug and be back friends with the adult who spanked me. I never wanted to be mad too long. Imagine being like that as a child. Those are not things that a parent really teaches you. Some things you are just born with. God has made you and chose you for whatever he has for you before you are born. He knows you in your mother's womb. He literally knows every strain of hair that is on your head. As I look back on my life as a sweet, lovable, innocent child, the love of God is more believable. I lived in a world full of wolves but to me life was so beautiful.

I really loved Sunday mornings because of my mom, she would fix us a nice big breakfast, bacon, eggs, grits and pancakes. I loved pancakes. After breakfast my mom, my sister and I would have "beauty day". Beauty day was when we would polish each other's nails, do our hair and just beautify ourselves while listening to the "Motown Sound", that is what my mother called it. We would listen to the music loud throughout the house while enjoying our Sunday.

I lived in West L.A as a younger child. I would love to go outside to play. In that area there were a few large hills. There was this one hill I liked to ride my bike to the top of slowly, and ride down really fast. It really was a dangerous hill to speed down, It was such a rush for me. I also would go to the freeway that we lived by, some of my friends and I would try to run across the freeway and back before the cars would come. If you are familiar with the freeways in California you will know the game that we were playing called, "Freeway" was a very dangerous game. I was so scared on this one particular day; I didn't really want to do it but peer pressure is real and my curiosity is also very real. So as my heart beat fast and then faster, I ran across the freeway as the cars were honking. I was so scared, but I made it back to the other side. What a rush!!

Well that scenario is how my life became, a rush, of highs and lows. The picture of my sunny days in California, of the smiles, candy, and happiness, paints the picture of my life. Not only that, the rush of doing something that I knew I was not supposed to do, also, is part of that same picture. Well I guess I have had a curious side since birth as well. Have you ever heard of the saying "curiosity killed the cat"? Hmm...Think about that.

CHAPTER 2

SHATTERED DREAMS

As I began to grow up I realized what I wanted to be when I grew up to be an adult. I wanted to be an actress. I wanted to be famous! Adults would ask me what I wanted to be when I grew up and I would put a big smile on my face and say. "An Actress".

Well I actually had that opportunity. I was able to be an actress in a McDonalds commercial when I was six years old. Out of all the kids in my acting class they chose me. Little me, chunky cheeks with a tooth missing, me. Yes! I thought, I am going to be in a commercial. Well the dream was shattered because the adults in my life decided that I could not do the commercial. I was totally heart broken. My destiny shattered! I wonder how my life would have been if I did that commercial? I guess I will never know. Well as I told you earlier in this book, I am not the type to ponder over unhappiness. So, I have thought about that a time or two, and then I let it go.

Part of the reason for me writing this book is to not only share my crazy life story but to let you know how I was actually able to get through all the ups and downs, and still be alive. I did not kill myself; I did not go to the streets and I never was on drugs. Do I deserve a cookie for that? No! I do deserve to be myself, share my story with you, and hopefully uplift and encourage you to get through the "mess" and keep it pushing."

Well, moving forward... After the commercial let down, I continued being a kid. I no longer had the dream of being an actress because that did not seem realistic any longer. I decided I wanted a family. I wanted to wait for marriage, have a husband, and children. Some of that idea came from the people that I started to be around.

My mom got married again. The first time since her and my father. I now had a stepdad in my life and most of the people at my place of worship were married at a young age and some already had children.

Coming from a woman as of today, I could say that if your child wants to do something, you should completely back them up in that. You cannot shelter a child from the world that they are going to have to be in anyways. You see, the adults in my life felt that a commercial would be too much for a small child, that the life of television was too much for children to go through. From my experience, as you will see when you continue to read this book, life is going to bring challenges regardless of what field or career you decide to take. So parents SUPPORT YOUR KIDS DREAM.

As I began to grow up and my family moved out of Los Angeles to the suburbs. I had friends of all races and ethnicities. I was well grounded as far as seeing many different cultures and ways of life. California is a melting pot full of all different kinds of people. I did not grow up with any prejudice in me of any sort, I am very grateful that I was raised in Southern California because it really taught me plenty about life, good and not so good.

I started to develop and notice boys. I had two best friends and both of them were Caucasian. My closest friend Jane and I were like Batman and Robin. We went everywhere together. We had fun together and we even got into trouble together. She was fair skin with freckles and she came from a really big family. I loved her parents and she loved mine. I am a brown skin girl, about 5"2 with curly hair. It never was a problem as it seems to be today with racism. I really did not notice anything like that, my mind was not in that direction.

I had so much fun getting dressed up to go to the movies with my friends. Talk about boys but never really did anything. My friends and I were really not fast girls. We were just kids wanting to have fun and I was enjoying life. We would dress up with our

Michael Jackson leather jackets and neon socks. One of my best friends had a swimming pool. We would go to her house and get in the pool and play marco-polo, she had a large family and they treated me just like family. She left a huge impact on my life because good friends are hard to find and sometimes outside people can become more like family then your own family. You are born in a family of people that you cannot choose, You can choose your friends in life. Choose wisely.

After middle school I was moved to another city where life changed a bit for me. I found myself in a situation that I was raped and the sacred life of waiting for marriage was thrown out the window. I did not have anyone to talk to and I felt like I did not have anyone to trust. I was sexually assaulted by someone that I knew which was the hardest part about my situation. It was more of the trust issue. I started to feel like I had nobody to trust. I was not with my friends that I felt the most comfortable with and I was thrown into the cage with the wolves. I wonder if my life as an actress would have been better. Who knows, life is always a challenge in one way or another and for me this was only the beginning.

After being sexually assaulted I found myself on the streets . I moved out of my house because I was no longer comfortable with living under the same roof as people that were in my house. I felt so alone. I could not talk to my parents because my mom had gotten a divorce from my step-dad and started dating other men. My communication with my mom was not there anymore. So I became a teenage run-away. I ran away and lived on the streets. I lived in different homes. Friends that I had recently met, they treated me nice, and we had some good times. They let me sleep at their house as a runaway, but it was not like my best friend that I trusted and grew up with. I moved from that area and I never saw my best friends again. It hurt and everything felt so different. I totally lost myself. I started to learn how to detach from things very well at a young age. I was able to detach from my parents, I detached from my best friends, and I detached from my home.

After I had become a runaway child, I started running wild, hanging around the wrong crowd in the projects at different friend's houses, my life was a mess. My only gateway was listening to music. I loved music. It was so calming. Especially the oldies. I would go to school and go back to my friend's house, grab our snacks and go in her room and listen to music.. On this one particular day while upstairs in my friends house, I heard her mom asking me to come downstairs. I ran downstairs and she had a talk with me. That is when she told me that my aunt was there to take me to Ohio to be with my dad. Her mom was so gentle and kind with me. She spoke to me in a way that made me feel better. She said "This may really be the best thing for you to do". So at the moment I made up my mind that I was going to willingly go to Ohio. Ohio where my father lived. My father, who I had not seen since I was a baby except for pictures. My mom moved me from him at the young age of two years old. I have heard several stories about that situation from both parents (each parent has a bit of a different story). Whatever the real story is, I was on my way!

CHAPTER 3

PIVOTAL MOMENTS

I was put on a flight to Ohio where my dad would be waiting at the airport to meet me. I had this one picture in my mind. It was a picture of my father in an army uniform. I was hoping I would be able to recognize him on sight when I got there. I saw one guy that I thought might be him, as I came closer, I realized I was mistaken. I looked around, from left to right, I did not see my dad. My stomach was nervous inside, as I anticipated what it would be like to see him. I started to relax and I stopped looking. I said to myself, "don't worry he will see you and come to you, he will recognize you. Just as I said that to myself, I looked across the terminal, there was absolutely no doubt in my mind who he was. My dad! I looked just like him! As soon as I saw him, I gave him a hug. I had been picturing this moment in my head for my lifetime. When I saw him, it was like meeting a stranger for the first time, but at the same time, it felt like I knew him. I had been let down by every man in my life that meant something to me so I naturally had my guards up when I met my father.

When I first arrived in Cleveland I moved in with my aunt, she was the one that came to get me. I took the flight to Cleveland with her.. She did not live in the house, but her two sisters did. It was ok for a little while. That didn't last long. I wanted to live with my dad. Problem was, he had a girlfriend that he knew from his past. She was a girlfriend that he dated on and off for years. This woman was much older than my dad, my opinion, she always looked mean. She could dress very well. I walked in her house and it was really nice. Everything was expensive in her house. She owned a four unit building and it was fully rehabbed with marble floors and countertops. I wanted to live there with my dad. She never accepted me. She said that she was jealous of me and my dad's relationship and that I could not live with her.

I was really enjoying having a father. When my dad was around we had good times together. We listened to music in the car and sang together. I always felt so safe when he was around, My dad bought me a pair of tennis shoes and I was on cloud nine. I realize now how much a daughter really needs her father. A "man figure" to show them love. When a girl does not have a father in her life, she seeks attention from a man to feel that emptiness that she never had by not having a father around. You may have heard in conversation the saying that a girl or woman has "daddy issues". Well, that is the meaning. Basically, when a woman seeks validation or comfort from a man because she never had the love from her own father. Those women usually end up hurt by a man before they realize the real problem. Because sometimes they find themselves looking for love in all the wrong places. Well, as happy as I was to have a strong and kind man around that told me I was beautiful, and reminded me that I was a queen, that feeling did not last for long. His jealous girlfriend did everything in her power to keep me away. So, I had to live with my grandmother, who is my dad's mom.

She was a beautiful woman with long black, shiny hair, high cheekbones and a beautiful creamy light brown skin tone. She looked like the pictures that you see of the Cherokee Indians in books. My grandmother had a really great sense of humor. She made me laugh a lot and she always said" You need to put some meat on your bones girl!" She always fed me soul food like greens, and cornbread. Her favorite in the morning was Grits. Growing up in LA I really didn't eat big breakfast every day, maybe on Sundays but during the other days of the week we ate Cereal. So my grandma thought I was a skinny little L.A girl that needed food (haha). She really tried to make me feel comfortable and I was getting there. The problem was I had a ball of confusion going on in my head. Being displaced from the only place I knew, which was California and being sent to Ohio, a completely different place was already a bit of a culture shock. Now I can't live with my dad because I am not wanted there. So I have to live with my

Grandmother that I was starting to get to know again and love. But I just was not feeling good about any of this, I could not adapt, and I really wanted to go back home. I loved California and I would ask every time I called back home to please let me come back home! She said No. So I finally stopped asking and realized I had to adapt and put my big girl panties on as they say and take care of myself.

I ran away from my grandma's house. I was not accustomed to the lifestyle that I was in and it was hard to adapt without my father there. All I really wanted was him there, I feel like love helps people to adapt to situations that may feel a little uncomfortable. My dad is a great guy and he always has been, he was going through substance abuse at the time so he could not be his best version of himself, as he is today. I understand that now as an adult. At the time I did not understand any of it and I did not care. So I ran away from home. Just like I did when I was in California. I found myself in the cold streets of Cleveland. Living with a new friend that I found from the school that I attended. I really liked this girl and she taught me a lot about the streets of Cleveland. But I barely knew her and that got old as well.

My grandmother on my mother's side of the family let me come to live with her. I grew up around my Grandmother and I loved her so much. She always came to California to see us during my years of growing up. I remember coming to Cleveland one time with my family to see her as well, when I was a teenager for a short period of time. Moving in with her was a little more familiar to me. It made me feel like I was closer to home. I was so happy that she took me in and gave me my own room. She really took good care of me. Grandmother worked a lot and could not babysit a teenager. She may have been a Grandmother but she was still dating and a jazzy lady. She was short and pretty with curly hair and golden brown skin. .My grandmother said she was "Brown Sugar" and she always told me I was too. She always told me" Baby, God made you just right, you have a little bit of everything which makes a complete package" She said" Grand momma is brown sugar and so are you". Then she would giggle. She had the cutest giggle. I wish I could hear that giggle sometimes, but now she is gone. Funny I can still hear that giggle in my head. I learned a lot from the woman that raised me but I really learned so much Pivotal information that would make me into the woman that I am today from my Grandmother Sue. I had to be independent because my grandmother did not believe in micro-management. She felt like once she told you the rules that you should do and respect them.

I knew I had to go to school near my Grandmother's house. I must admit it was a struggle going to school in Cleveland Ohio especially being the "new girl from California" That's all I ever heard. I would walk down the halls and hear the students whispering to each other saying,, " That's that new girl from California." Some people liked me and others could not stand me, for absolutely no reason and some didn't like me because all the boys liked the new girl from California, which so happened to be me. I was asked lots of questions about the lifestyle in California. At the time NWA, Too Short the rapper, Dr Dre, and Snoop dogg were out. The west coast was the hottest place to be on the map and Cleveland was nothing like it. As a matter of fact no other state at that time could touch the west coast in regards to excitement. It was just an exciting place to live and I had questions asked about how it is in California, all day at school.

As I was meeting new friends and trying to accept that I am not going back home to California. I met a guy that I thought I was in love with. This was my first time ever feeling like I was really in love. Problem was he was nine years older than me and I was just a teenager.. Well what happens next is just a continuation of the cycle. Hold on to your rail because the roller coaster ride continues.

CHAPTER 4

IGNORING THE RED FLAGS

As I was meeting new friends and trying to accept that I am not going back home to California. I met a guy that I fell head over heels about. This guy was much older than me. Me and my girls were at a high school basketball game, he came up to us with his friends. I started talking to him. I liked him but at the time another one of our friends liked him also. After we got to know each other we finally decided to go on a date alone. He took me out to dinner and the movies. He really treated me well. I had never had a real relationship like that before. He was nine years older than me. So of course I was sprung on the idea of being taken care of and showed a life that I never had. He had lots of money and really nice cars. He really took care of me. I had new clothes, lots of jewelry, and some of his time. I was on cloud nine.

Then shortly after, I started to realize that I was always getting into arguments and fights about this man, with other females that he was messing around with. They would call my phone and even come to my house.. He was a ladies man. He took great care of me financially, but at the same time he had other girls hanging around him. We started dating, I was falling for his charm when I started realizing he was cheating on me..

One night he came to pick me up at my grandmother's home., which is where I was still living. My Grandmother was very much up on the games that men play. She also was a young mother and had been in bad relationships with street men and ladies men, the same cycle, some call it a generational curse.. So that made it very easy for her to see right through him. She was not happy the night that she met him. She said that he was too old for me. She was drilling him with questions and I was so embarrassed that I said something disrespectful to her, she said" Aren't you too old to be dating my granddaughter, why don't you date someone your own age"?" I told my grandmother to please mind her business, then I went on to say," I love him and he loves me." She struck me over the head with a wooden dough rolling pen. I was so embarrassed and afraid of losing someone that I finally felt loved . I ran out the house down the street crying. He caught up with me and said I love you, but you have to respect your grandmother. He left and I left with him, leaving my grandmother heart broken.

As we kept sneaking around dating, I ended up getting pregnant when I was really young, still a minor. Now, I am about to be a teenage, unmarried mom.

I started cutting classes in school so much during that time period, because I was sick from being pregnant. My grandmother did not know that I was pregnant. Everyday when she went to work I would get dressed to go to school, as soon as she left for work, I would come back home most days and go back to bed because I was having horrible morning sickness. I was afraid at first to tell her that I was pregnant. I knew how disappointed she would be. She had so much faith in me. My grandmother always said, "Granddaughter you are not like these other hood girls, you are not a street girl, you grew up with class". I was so afraid to tell her I was pregnant, so I was just dealing with it alone.

In the meantime, I was having trouble with girls at the school wanting to fight me. I told my uncle about the incident with the girls wanting to jump on me at the school and he gave me a pocket knife. He told me that fighting is not fair. He said, "Niece when you fight you are fighting to win." So I took his advice and ended up getting expelled for bringing a knife to school, because I was always getting jumped by other girls who did not like me.

One day a girl called me out to fight, she was with her group of friends, I already heard they planned to jump me. She said," You want to fight me?" and I said," What's up you want to fight me"? Although I really did not want to fight, I really refused to sound scared. Then she rushed towards me and all of her friends, it was about seven of them. I brought the knife to school that my uncle told me to carry. Cleveland was a really rough place, and those girls were ready to fight. All I could hear was my uncle's voice saying " It is not such a thing as fighting fair, you fight to win, and I stabbed her in the side of her face. The knife dropped and I was fighting about seven girls. All I remember is kicking, punching, screaming and going crazy. I was fighting for my life. The principal broke up the fight and I was expelled until the next year.

I saw one of the girls that I had a fight with at school a few days later. She was at the grocery store, she looked as if she saw a ghost. She told her friend to keep walking, that is that crazy girl, she shouted! My uncle said if I beat up the main girl, then everyone else would stop messing with me . Everyone has that one uncle in their family, like my Uncle Jimmy, that runs the streets, and has lots of stories to tell about how he beat up the entire block. Well this time my uncle was right about that, he knew how Cleveland was, because I did not have any problems with girls in Cleveland wanting to fight me anymore. I did have another set of problems; I was pregnant at 16 yrs old. I had finally told my grandma that I was pregnant. I was living with my grandmother for a few months, until one day she had a talk with me and she said that since I am pregnant that I am now grown, she told me that I had to move out before the baby was born.

My boyfriend moved me to a house where I lived on my own. just me and my pregnant belly... I was young, did not know much about life yet, in a real relationship, about to have a newborn baby. Trying to figure out how to take care of a new baby with no real adults around, I am not sure where my dad was. I do know that he experienced the sickness of drug abuse, again.. My mom was still in California and now she fell into the drug crises of the 80's, which was really bad in California, and started using drugs and alcohol as well. I thought to myself, at least I have my man and he is my baby's father. During my pregnancy he would stop by some times and take me to this delicious soul food restaurant, sometimes take me out to the movies. On many occasions I was up all night calling him and wondering where he was. He disappeared alot and sometimes for days. I just wanted him around because being pregnant and alone was no fun and he was taking care of me financially while I was pregnant. He convinced me that those girls who called my phone were just jealous and that he was not cheating, and I believed him. I never could see the writing on the wall. He cheated on me with different girls and his ex-girlfriend, while I was pregnant, and he got her pregnant as well. I had a very stressful pregnancy. My heart was broken.

My water broke and my baby's father was nowhere around. He wasn't at the hospital when I had my baby. Fortunately, I had people who cared about me. My grandmother was dating a Polish man. He was a really nice guy. He later became my grandad a few years later, they were married in Hawaii.. Both of them were there for me at the hospital when my baby was being born, I held his hand the whole time, squeezing it so tight that his hand went from white to red! He did not have any children of his own, so this was a new experience for him, I must say he did very well. I really miss him. Being around such a caring man really made me have some hope that there are still good men in this world. He was a white man, which is one of the reasons why I do not believe certain people of a certain race are all bad. It is the individual person.

I tried to make it work with my child's father. It was a challenge because the girls and women were not going away. He was a real ladies man, a real playboy. He had multiple baby mothers and it was always a new secret being revealed. I was young and he was older than me. I fell into his trap and found myself pregnant again. He ended up going to the federal penitentiary. I would catch a bus from Ohio to North Carolina with my child to visit him. Right before he was locked up I ended up finding out that I was pregnant again. I was very scared and confused about what to do, especially knowing that he was fighting a case and could go to jail. While catching buses alone to visit him in a strange town, I found out that another girl was doing the same thing. This woman was not even one of the girls that I knew about before he went to jail. In my mind and heart I knew that was my breaking point. Will this cycle ever end I thought? I asked him, how could you cheat on me and you are in jail. Is this possible? He said "Don't worry about her, she is taking care of me financially while I am here. You just take care of the kids". He was promising to marry me when he got home so I was faithfully waiting for him.

Meanwhile, after my baby boy was born, I looked into the eyes of my beautiful child and that is when I realized that I had to live right and depend on myself for my innocent children who depended on me. I started doing things for myself the right way, for the first time. I was working two jobs, I bought my first car, and I was raising my children at home by the age of eighteen... My children meant the world to me. I never wanted them to want anything. I was working two jobs and I was doing ok for myself and my family.

I never wanted my children to experience living in the projects or struggling. I had in my mind that they deserved so much more. I always put them before me, they were wearing name brand clothes and shoes when I wasn't even wearing them. I always put my innocent children first. They were just babies, and as a parent the mother and the father is all a helpless baby has. I wanted to protect them and be the best mom that I knew how to be. My mind triggered on when I was a child how happy I was, I wanted them to experience being happy.

Since my children's father ended up in jail. I was now a single parent. Working two jobs and long hours was too much, so I started coming apart at the seams because I was working too much, and tired. One night driving home late after my 3rd shift job at a warehouse, I fell asleep at the wheel. Fortunately, God was shining his light down on me and protected me. I woke up and I was in the middle of the street with cars zooming by me on all sides! I was terrified. I drove home and eased up on my work schedule.

I finally decided to leave my children's father alone. My uncle's girlfriend always would tell me that I deserve so much better. She always reminded me of how beautiful I was. She would ask me if I knew how beautiful I was. I would say yes, but deep inside sometimes I was not sure. So much drama and so many scars inside made me question my worth. If only I was the woman I am now, then. I told her I did not want to leave him when he was in jail because that is when he needed me the most. She looked at me and said "Now is the best time for you to leave him because you can give yourself time to get over him." She knew that it was hard for me to let go as long as he was home. I knew that he may not be the man for me, I just wanted it to work for my kids and he was my first love, my first real boyfriend. It was easy for me to let go the day that one of my friends called me and said, "Girl there is a girl named May that has a tattoo of your man's name on her." "She said, "he is her man, we saw her at the mall" My friends were like detectives when it came to me.! They managed to get the girl's phone number and I called her to ask her a few questions. Sure enough she also thought that she was in a relationship with him and she also has been going to North Carolina to see him. I was done after that. There was no way that I was going to continue waiting faithfully for a man that cheated on me constantly. I told my uncle's girlfriend that she was right, now is the best time for me to move on with my life. He called me that night and I broke up with him over the phone.

I asked my grandad on my mom's side of the family if I could give him rent and move in with him for a while. I was burnt out, realizing that if I kept burning myself out this way, it would be the death of me. Moving in with my real grandad was a challenge because he lived with his wife and some of her adult children that still lived at home. I loved my granddad and spending time with him was memorable. He was an awesome and amazing person. He was handsome, very fair skin with a long ponytail, really fine hair, tall, and very funny. He always had such a huge sense of humor. I loved him so much. I miss him. I remember riding in the car with him and my song from the group called "Escape" came on. The lyrics went" Kick off your shoes and relax your feet, party on down to the escape beat, just kick it.", well grandad decided to change the lyrics to, "kick off your shoes with your funky feet", (HAHA). Being around him was always memorable and good times.

My grandad was another great memory of a man in my life. He had married again, the woman that he was with had adult children which were my aunts and uncles, most of them were really nice but the house was a bit crowded for me and my two children. I really appreciated it, at the same time, I was thinking that I would not be there for long.

After living at my grandfather's house for a while, I started to go out sometimes with my aunt. She was a little older than me, she liked to hang out and have fun. I wasn't even twenty-one yet, but somehow, I managed to get in the club with her. So one night after one of our long days and nights of having fun, my aunt and I decided to go to the store. While in the line at the store a guy started talking to me, he told me he would buy me anything in the store that I wanted. I said all I wanted was what was already in my cart, so he paid for my groceries and asked for my phone number. I was a single mom of two and thinking I really didn't want to get into another relationship, so I told him, "Why don't you give me your number, and maybe I'll call you later."

So he told me his name was Raheem and he gave me his number. I took it home and didn't think much about it, but my auntie was with me when I met him and she was all over me to call him. She reasoned that if he had that kind of money and was willing to spend it on a stranger then he must be a good man and the kind of provider who could take care of me and my kids. Initially he didn't really seem like my type, he looked like he had just finished fixing cars, his clothes looked dirty, I just assumed that he was a mechanic, so I decided to call him and see what happened.

After a couple of days had passed, I called him and we ended up talking on the phone for hours. It seemed as if he wanted some of the things in life that I wanted. And we were really hitting it off over the phone.. We kept talking on the phone and he wound up almost telling me he loved me during one of those conversations, before we had even gone on a real date. That really threw me for a loop. Finally, I agreed to go out with him, he showed up to take me out in a really nice car with his own driver, which I hadn't seen outside of my stepfather back in California growing up. This time he was cleaned up, his clothes were nice and he smelled good. He had on a nice hoodie, nice jeans and a pair of Timberland boots. He picked me up in a nice car, cleaned and smelled good. He had a chauffeur, which I later found out was his friend. He really wanted to impress me. It worked in his favor. He treated me like a queen that night. We went out to a nice restaurant to eat. We were having a really nice conversation and everything seemed good so far. After dinner we went for a ride and he was playing one of my favorite CD's at the time. Toni Braxton. I loved her music. It was a great night. He laid his head on my lap and asked me to rub his head. I rubbed his head and then he said, " I really had a good time with you, I do not want this night to end, would you like to go to Las Vegas?" I had never been to Las Vegas before, so I said yes, why not. I barely knew anything about this guy,, but it just felt right. I felt like this guy is saying all the right things and he is doing all the right things and I am single with two kids and a baby father in Jail. What do I have to lose? Well, I had to learn the hard way, that patience and getting to know someone better is the best thing to do. Because people will eventually show their true colors. The mask will come off.

We drove to a hotel and I made it clear to him that we can hang out but I am not having any sexual relations with you, I said. . I told him that if I go to Vegas with him it will be on the terms of..no strings attached. He said that is perfectly ok. He said " I like you and you are going to be my girl". I can't lie, I wasn't against the thought of being his girl either. While at the hotel watching T.V. and planning for the Vegas flight, He said I have to leave, I will be right back. I had snacks and soda, in a nice hotel away from my Grandad's house where multiple people lived. Why not stay and wait? So,that is what I did. I was lounging, watching T.V. and enjoying myself. I must have fallen asleep because hours later I heard a knock on the door. It was him. I looked at the time and it was morning. I said what about Vegas? I was upset because he left me in the hotel room all night alone and I had fallen asleep and it was morning. We went shopping and I had to go home to check on my kids and pay the babysitter. He gave me some money to pay the babysitter and off we went to Las Vegas for an overnight trip. Everything was nice in Las Vegas.

Unfortunately, I would learn that he was a hustler and he liked to gamble and be in the streets just like my last boyfriend who was the father of my kids. I remember thinking to myself, why can't I ever find a nice, normal guy to like me, that I also like back? That seemed to be a cycle that I could not break at the time. My praying and love for God was always within me and a part of my life. It just was not my daily way of life, like it is today. Because if it was, the holy spirit would have caused me to discern that I was on the same path leading to the same cycle.

He was not as old as my kids dad, just a few years older than me. He always had money and he did not mind spending it on me and my children. I never had to ask for anything, he would just take care of things without asking, and that was attractive to me, especially because I was raising my kids and doing everything financially by myself.

He said that I was not like the other girls out there, he liked the fact that I would work and make my own way by myself. He said that is the reason that he does so much for me, because I never really ask. He said that he realized that I was really different when my car broke down and I did not ask him for help to fix it. I worked extra hours at work and got it fixed by myself. I was accustomed to money so my outlook on it was different from other females. He said that I was not a gold digger just looking to take all of his money, and he liked that about me. I felt like I could finally be on a team with someone and it felt good. He asked me to move in with him, and I did. Not realizing that he was living with another woman that he had children with. I kept asking him If I could go to his house, not knowing that I could never go to his house because he moved his kids' mother in a house downstairs from his own mother. I said" How was I supposed to move in with you if you are living with another woman" ? Of course he said that they were over. He explained that he walked in the barber shop and the guys were playing a video tape of a woman having sex with the customer, that woman was his woman, his kids mother. He found out that she was cheating and he just did not want to put her out with his children, because she did not have anywhere to go. He had been with her since she was a teenager and they had two kids. I believed him and that was actually one of the things that he did not lie about.

. First, we were staying at an extended stay hotel room together. Which is when the red flags really started. I had already seen a few prior to this incident that I tried to overlook. However, this incident was not one that I could make an excuse for. I remember him getting angry because I questioned him about his baby's mother, so he took the chicken, macaroni salad and greens that he had just purchased and threw them across the hotel room at me. I saw a side of him that I had not seen, I thought to myself that I need to leave. As I was getting my things to leave, he grabbed me and said that he was sorry. He said that he just does not like hearing about her. He made it up to me by doing and saying all the right things. He really knew how to make up well. I was thinking that I was in too deep. I can't leave now, is what I said. He said he is sorry and he will never do it again. So I stayed. I just forgave him for his outrage because I didn't want to think that he had an anger problem.

After staying in the extended stay for a few months we rented my grandmother's house. We later bought it from her, fixed it up, and then flipped it for a profit. That was our first taste of Real Estate Investing. Which was a business that we ultimately went into together. He proposed to me on our first Valentine's day together. I said yes and I was excited about my life. We were having good times and he had not shown any more anger for a few months. He took me on another trip to Las Vegas, just him and I. In the same year. I thought I was on top of the world, I was rolling around the city in nice cars, getting spoiled with money and gifts. I thought I was finally happy. He made me feel like we were a family. A family is something I always longed for since I was a child. Besides ALL OF THE RED FLAGS that I ignored. I was finally happy!

CHAPTER 5

TYPES OF ABUSE & IPV (INTIMATE PARTNER VIOLENCE)

> *"Emotional Abuse/ Psychological Abuse- includes non-physical behaviors that are meant to control, isolate, or frighten you. This may present in romantic relationships as threats, insults, constant monitoring, excessive jealousy, manipulation, humiliation, intimidation, and dismissiveness, among others." "National Domestic Violence Hotline"*

Emotional Abuse

I was going through some emotional abuse from him. I let it go because I wanted a happy life for me and my kids. I remember one day in particular. It was hard to ignore, he told one of his friends to go and get a paper bag, he put the bag up to my face, in front of one of his friends, he said, "she just barely made it". I was like,

"What are you talking about, what cut?" I said frantically, with an attitude in my voice. He laughed and said "You just barely made it because I usually only date light skinned girls." I just made the cut because I was not as dark as the paper bag. I knew at that moment that he was sick. Especially when he was dark skinned.

Looking back and analyzing things today, I realized that he did not like his own self. His mother was dark, his father was dark and one of his baby's mothers was much darker than me. It sounds to me that he wanted to pass his cycle of insecurities down to me. When I asked him, "How could you judge my color, when I am a caramel brown woman and you have children with a very dark skin woman"? His excuse was he was young then, but moving forward, he only talks to light skin girls. All of that is abuse. Mental abuse, to break me down in thinking that I am just barely enough. I was so worried about getting a summer tan because If I got a little darker, I would not be liked by him, or he would not find me attractive anymore.

Emotional abuse is so bad because it stays with you longer than physical abuse. The scars are deeper and they never really completely go away. It makes you question your worth over a period of time. I never even thought about color, I always knew I was beautiful. No man or woman had ever said anything like that to me in my entire life. I was so confused and started to question myself. I still stayed. Looking back I guess I felt it was not enough to make me leave.

> *"Physical Abuse & Intimate Partner Violence (IPV)- Intimate partner violence (IPV) is domestic violence by a current or former spouse or partner in an intimate relationship against the other spouse or partner. IPV can take a number of forms, including physical verbal, emotional, economic and sexual abuse." "Wikipedia"*
>
> *"Physical abuse is any intentional act causing injury or trauma to another person or animal by way of bodily contact. In most cases, children are the victims of physical abuse, but adults can also be victims." "Wikipedia"*

Physical abuse

Shortly after that incident, I got my first glimpse of the darker, meaner side of him, the side that in my heart of hearts I think I had just been waiting to see emerge, based on his temper from time to time. I just wasn't expecting it to be this bad.

Mental, psychological & physical abuse

It was a cold night in Cleveland, freezing outside. He was not home and it was getting late. I needed to go to the grocery store. I had called him before going. He was not responding to me. So I made my way to the store alone. My car was in the shop and I needed a ride back home,, I had bought food for dinner and for the rest of the week. I called him but he was too busy to come get me when I called. So I told him I would call a friend for a ride instead. He went insane with jealousy, he said" are you going to call a man for a ride"?. I honestly told him I didn't really know who I was going to call yet, but it wasn't a big deal.. It will not be a man. I just needed to get home. I heard it in his voice that he was angry. So I said, "do not worry, It will not be a man". But I could hear it in his voice, he did not believe me, so he told me to wait there and he would send his driver, who was also his cousin, to come pick me up. So after grocery shopping I checked out, went outside while waiting to be picked up.

His cousin came all along, he was not in the car with him. He picked me up and dropped me off at home. I was asking his cousin where he was and he did not have a clue. I walked in the house and brought in the bags.. After putting up the food I was upstairs unwinding, I heard him come in the door downstairs. I was getting ready to go downstairs to greet him. I could not even make it downstairs because he came literally running upstairs... He ran up the stairs wearing some of the brown steel-toed Timberland boots that men wear when they're working outside. He caught sight of me and swung his leg all the way back and brought it forward straight into my shin. All I saw were the guts of the meat of my leg splattering in all directions. I am a girly girl, I am 5"2 and I was slim and petite with curves, he was 6"0 and husky, and that kind of pain was nothing like I had ever felt before, and I was screaming and hollering. He just stood there watching me writhe in agony and pain. He wouldn't even take me to the hospital. I had never been in a fight with anyone before that I felt that much pain, I had never seen that much blood and guts gushing out of my leg. As I hollered he just acted as if he didn't care.

I was shocked to see how cold hearted he can get. I should've just left then, but where would I go? I felt as if I was in too deep. We had a home together, we were starting a family and business, my kids did not need anything financially and I did not have to worry about stressing over taking care of them alone with no father. I finally had a man of my own and my kids had a father, I thought to myself. I had already been through so much at such a young age. I did not know my worth anymore. The mental abuse of feeling like you just made the cut, your family doesn't want you and this is the best that there is. These were feelings of a young woman that was bruised mentally and physically. That was my first time seeing his temper come out like that, but unfortunately, it wouldn't be the last.

That was the beginning of the cycle of violence. My babies were little, and he started putting his hands on me whenever I did something he perceived as being wrong. I would pack my clothes after a beating, I was ready to leave him, but as soon as I got to the door, he would show up. He would take my bags back into the house and tell me that we could talk things out, he said that he would not hit me anymore, until it started sounding like a song.. He was hitting me, cheating on me, and I was so tired of him, I was trying so hard to just raise my kids the right way, that I never let them know what was going on. I had gotten to the point that

I wanted to just leave him! This was only the first year. . But he wouldn't let me leave.

After we had been together a while, someone close to me who lived out of state wanted to come and visit us, I said OK.. She had heard about my lavish lifestyle and wanted to come out to see me. When I told him that she was coming, he got really interested and asked what she looked like and started acting like he was going to be very flirtatious around her, saying that she was going to want him. She came to town and she looked beautiful, but I found out later that she had gotten addicted to drugs. She was hiding it well, looking great on the outside but it was twisting her up on the inside. She arrived at my house and everything was great. I was very happy to see her and spend time with her. I had a great love for her and I had really missed California. She reminded me of home, which to me California was home. She and I had been talking about me going back to visit her and my family. She did not know what I was going through. I wanted to get away from him for a while and figure out what to do next. I was very interested in the idea of going. Everything was going great until one day, she asked me to ask him if he could drop her off somewhere in the middle of the day. I didn't see any harm in it because I trust her and had major respect for her. I told her no problem. When he came back home, I told him that I was planning on going out of town with her, he told me point blank, "She tried to have sex with me." I started crying and yelling at him, I was saying "You are lying, she would never do that to me," because she was someone that I really trusted and loved, but he shot me down and told me that she had tried to touch him inappropriately and even tried to touch his area with her mouth, in the car earlier when he dropped her off.. He was now adding mental and psychological abuse to the mix, when it came to dealing with me. He told me, "I'm sorry nobody loves you," but I love you, I am the only one that loves you." He said that he feels sorry for me that I don't have anyone to love me and that I would be stupid to go visit someone like that. Then he went on to say." you better not mention this to her." I was like," why can't I mention it to her? He said because she knows where we live and she might get mad. He was insinuating that she seems like a vindictive person. He said If you mention it to her, you and I will have a problem. Once again, I was being told not to tell anyone because if I did, I would also have to deal with the consequences.

When she came back to our house, I couldn't even talk to her, I looked at her face with filthy disgust and hurt. I didn't know If I wanted to scream and cry or fight her.. Out of all the people in the world I just never thought that she would be the one to betray me, she was someone I looked up to. We had even been talking about me leaving and going back to California with her, all of her and I conversations were racing and replaying through my head. At the same time I still did not completely believe him.

After realizing that I was not talking to her while she was in my house. She called someone that she knew that lived in town to come and pick her up, so she left my house again. When she left for a while, I did not know where she was. He had also left. When he came back home, he made me make love with him while torturing me mentally by talking about her while we were in bed together. He was saying things to make me think that when she left my house the second time with her friend, that she called him and they met up. I was confused and hurt because I did not know what to believe or think and she was acting suspicious. It would have been easy just to ask her, except he made me promise not to mention it to her. How could someone be so evil? I cried to him and said why are you doing this to me, do you hate me? I said if you hate me just leave me alone and let me leave. He said," no, I love you and I want you to know the type of person that she is so that you will never want to leave me and go with her again, I am the only one that loves you." After that, I retreated to the tub, about the only place I could seem to find solace when something went wrong. I felt like I had a nervous breakdown then. I cried and pulled my hair in the tub and I screamed out loud, "Why Me"! I cried and cried until my head started to hurt. It hurt so bad I had thoughts of just leaving this earth. I knew that I had something to live for, my small children who needed me. Then the thought of ending the pain went away, I had to calm myself down. I was finally able to calm myself down and prayed for clarity. I prayed for God to help me deal with this hurt. The betrayal of getting hurt by someone close to you that you trust, stabbed like a knife in my back and only God could fix it, and he did, but the grace of God. I pulled the pieces that I had left of me back together, and put a smile on my face.

The day she was leaving to go back home I still couldn't talk to her, she started asking me over and over what was wrong with me and why I wasn't even going to say goodbye to her. Finally, I said, "You know what you did, and you're horrible." I looked her in the face with tears in my eyes because at that point, I knew he was telling the truth, and I said to her you are really horrible, I can't believe you did this to me, I trusted you.. She didn't say anything except, "What, what did I do? She just left and as she was leaving she said "I could die or anything on my trip back home and you are treating me like this," That was some real narcissistic behavior that she had. I was in the house with two narcissistic people. I didn't talk to her for a long while. But I stayed with him, for whatever reason.

A year or so later, I went to the doctor, and the doctor told me that I was pregnant. I was so happy because he kept sweating me to get pregnant, he even would say, "What is wrong with you, why can't you get pregnant. "I was not really in a rush to have another child, I already had two and he was already showing his true colors. Once I found out I was pregnant I was happy, thinking to myself maybe this will complete our blended family. Maybe this is the one thing that will make him happy and he will act right.

It started off nice, he was buying me all kinds of clothes and making sure I ate all the different foods that I liked. He was really spoiling me while I was pregnant. I loved ice-cream and crab-legs during the beginning of my pregnancy. He always made sure that I had whatever I wanted to eat even if he came home late. He would walk through the door with what I asked for. Before I was pregnant he had already bought me a beautiful diamond ring and proposed to me. He asked me to marry him on valentine's day. It was very sweet. I would think back how we were in the room at our new home and he went down on one knee, looked up at me so sweetly and said I want you to marry me. Of course I said ok, I wanted a family. Everything seemed to be going ok, I couldn't see anything else going wrong.

Until one day while I was around five months pregnant, I remember my now fiancé at the time, had another girl hanging around at our house whom he said was a friend of his from school. He said she can help you while you are pregnant. She befriended me and we were getting along, but all the while he was cheating on me with her. I had suspicions that were confirmed one day when he invited me to go to Las Vegas with him. He also invited her to go as well. I was around five months pregnant. I did not find out she was going until we were there and she popped up at the hotel where we were staying. I was feeling really good before she came to the room because he had gotten my hair done and I had a beautiful new burgundy dress with Versace Heels on and new diamond jewelry. He and I were going to a Mike Tyson Fight. Everybody was in Vegas at that time. Although I was feeling down when she knocked on the door, I made the best of the situation and tried to keep a smile on my face.. He called her over to me and asked her to pull up my dress. I was shocked at what was going on. He told her to touch me and she did it. He said to her "don't she have some pretty breasts." She was like yes. I was like, Boy what is going on? I am pregnant and I do not want to do any of this." He had never acted like this before. I asked him right then if they ever messed around and they both said no. He and I had never done anything like that before so I was upset, thinking that they had been messing around. I was tired and pregnant so I left the thought alone. Although it lingered in the back of my mind.

We took a limo to the fight and as we were getting into the limo a group of guys was like, "damn you look good baby. We all thought they were talking to the other girl, his friend that was with us. The last person I thought they were talking to was me, for me to have been pregnant my stomach was not huge, but, at the same time, you could definitely tell that I was with child. but when she turned around they were like not you, the pretty one with the burgundy dress on. He got so furious and squeezed my hand and started telling them that I was his girl and pulling me along to get in the car, meanwhile the guys were arguing with him. I could tell they were from L.A because of the way that they were talking. He was saying to me, "See, that is why I do not like bringing you nowhere.." Crazy because even though he was no good for me, I hated to see them have to beat him up that day. So I got in the argument and was like please stop.! " Also, not knowing if he would switch it around tonight and make me have to pay for how they were acting. The girl that he was cheating on me with was not even attractive, she did have a huge butt. . When a man cheats it is sometimes nothing that you do wrong. You can be a great woman to him and you can be attractive. If Halle Berry got cheated on and she was known as the most beautiful actress at one time, then anybody can, as far as I am concerned. I am glad I was able to calm that situation down because she was standing there looking lost and I was mentally disturbed to try and stop someone from beating up a man that abuses me. But he and I really needed God, we just did not know it then.

His physical abuse continued even while I was pregnant. We went back home and things continued to get worse, as my stomach continued to grow.. Once we were having an argument about him going out of town and taking a girl that I knew liked him, he claimed that she was going along for her other friends. I asked him why I cannot come along as well? He said that I was pregnant. I said "well, if I am pregnant, and you know that this girl likes you, she calls my house playing on my phone and asking for you, knowing that she is irritating me. Why would you put that stress on me? I felt like he should not go and I said it. He pushed me, and I fell down the stairs but fortunately there was no damage to the baby, although I had to be on bedrest for a period of time..

While still pregnant with my daughter and still on bedrest, now I am about eight months pregnant. We had another incident that made me say I am done this time. While at home on a winter night the kids were at the babysitters and I was cooking gravy and steak for him. He was going on and on to his friend about his Ex-wife, the one that he caught cheating on him . I said under my breath, "I hate when he talks about her." Well he heard me and he decided it was time to shut me up, so he came over and started punching me in the face. He kept on doing it until his friend finally told him to stop. My nose was bleeding and my lip was busted. There was blood all over the floor and hot gravy splashed all over the kitchen. I had every reason to feel insecure about his ex-wife and mother of his other children, because she would come around and she was still sleeping with him sometimes and always found a way to make it known. She knew about our engagement and the baby on the way. She was pretending that she was trying to be my friend. He was like the devil, but I couldn't get away from him.

CHAPTER 6

ALWAYS FIGHTING FOR MY LIFE

I remained on bedrest because the doctor said that I was under stress, I knew why but sadly the doctor did not. I had a beautiful, healthy baby girl! She was shown so much love from my side of the family as well as his. I just knew that she would keep everything together. He was there with me when she was born. I was so happy because I never got a chance to experience my baby's father being there for the birth of my child. He seemed like he was really happy and he thought our baby was so beautiful. On the last day of my stay at the hospital, before I was scheduled to come home, he brought a girl to the hospital with him. The girl was the same female he said he knew since he was in school, yes, the same female that he took to Las Vegas with us. He claimed that he was not messing around with her and that he saw our baby. I could not believe what I was seeing and hearing. I tried to believe him because I really did not have the energy to not believe him. I did not want that craziness to stop me from feeling the joy of having my baby.

When I came home from the hospital, he had cleaned the house and had a delicious steak dinner waiting for me. I later found out a few days later, the house was cleaned up by his "old friend from school", I guess he had her clean up. Wow, as I write this book I realize how much I went through. I really hope you are feeling this book and living this drama. I hope you are saying" this girl had to be crazy to stay with him"? Because if you are saying that, then I know that this book is working. Keep reading because it gets worse before it gets better.

One night after he and I had our daughter, I decided to get out and enjoy the night with my cousins. We all drove my car, me and my two cousins, I had a gold Lexus at the time with gold rims, so all my cousins and friends wanted to ride with me. We pulled up to the club and went in and began drinking and listening to music. I received a phone call a few minutes later from my husband. He said," Are you at the club with your ex-boyfriend?" " I said no I am with my cousins, I told you we were going." He said, " I see your ex-boyfriend's car outside, I am outside, come out now!" I was nervous because he really seemed mad. I honestly did not see the guy's car outside, and he was not my ex-boyfriend. He really was a guy that liked me when we were in high school. My husband just knew that the guy liked me and we talked briefly while in school, but nothing serious, he actually lived around the corner so he really could have been anywhere, It was a neighborhood bar and lounge. Nervously I walked outside. When I went outside I saw the car but I did not see the guy. I said maybe that is someone's car that looks like his. He said no it is his, get in the car! I said what about my cousins? They drove here with me? He said, "leave your car here, that way your cousins can get home, get in the car with me". I went inside and gave my keys to my cousins and made them aware that I was leaving. I tried to smile and make them think that everything was ok, while inside I was so scared.

We got in the car together and arrived home, he sat me on the coach and his exact words were, "Everybody thinks that pretty little Kim is so cute, well I am about to mess your face up". He started punching me and busted my nose and my lip open. Then he grabbed me and dunked my face in our Jacuzzi hot tub. He tried to drown me by grabbing my neck and dunking my head in the water, he held it there for a few minutes, and then lifted it up, he dunked it again, and held my head under the water for a few minutes and lifted my head up again. After doing that about three times the fourth time he held my head under the water even longer until I could not hold my breath any longer, my body started to get limp, I was trying to splash the water to let him know I was dying, I believed I stopped kicking, at that point he lifted me up for air. As I gasped for air, coughing and choking I said to myself, he is going to kill me tonight, I better get out of here! So, I ran and busted through the front door and started running down the street and hollering, "Please somebody help me please, he is going to kill me." It was dark and not a single soul stopped to help me. He was chasing me down the street. He finally caught up with me and covered my mouth with his hand. He tried lifting me up off the ground as I was still kicking and screaming get off of me, he told me to shut up or he will really fuck me up. He said that he would not hurt me anymore tonight if I would be quiet. He asked me to please be quiet because he was afraid to go to jail. He dragged me into the house and told me to go wash my face that was full of blood. As I washed my face, I was looking at my small framed face that I did not recognize in the mirror. I remember putting my head in the water to wash my face but looking behind me afraid that he would bash my face in the sink. My lip was busted open, my eyes were black, the blood vessels in my neck were broken, as I looked at my face in the mirror, I began to cry harder. I could not believe this was my life. The man that I loved, taking care of me financially, the man who I thought I had a home with, just could not stop beating on me. He could not stop and realize that I was a person, a human being just like his mother. I was heartbroken and really ready to give up. I felt like I was really sleeping with the enemy. It was something about me that made him jealous. If a man is jealous of your natural glow, there is nothing you can do to fix that, but leave. That night he made me have sex with him against my will. I cried the entire time. Every stroke made me feel nauseous. On the surface, we looked like the perfect urban couple. Attractive, in business together, doing huge profits flipping houses all over Cleveland and surrounding areas. I helped to run the company and the house while he made sure the contracting work was complete and handled getting new contracts.

By the time I got pregnant again by him with our second child, we were millionaires. We were living in the Rockefeller area of Ohio and had a huge house that we had fully renovated, with a four-car garage. Business was going very well, we learned from some Indians that lived in Ohio how to flip on a larger scale, by using OPM (other people's money). We were not only rehabbing homes in Cleveland, we began to get involved with new home construction. We were really doing great in the public's eyes, but he was still sleeping with other people every chance he got. He had so much money that people all over town knew him and respected him because of his money. We were considered "hood rich at first and then we moved up to be simply upper class.".

With all of that financial success I still was not happy. Yes, I had my moments of happiness. Being around my children brought me happiness. Taking my step children, my children, my little sister and younger cousins to amusement parks, having big parties with jumpers and ponies, all of those things is what made me happy. Everyone would come to my house for BBQ's and holiday dinners, not only was my house large and always in a nice area, my house was fun! I let the kids be kids, I loved children and seeing the babies happy was life for me. Holiday dinners I would cook large soul food meals, even my grandmother liked to come over for those dinners, I loved having my grandmother, her husband, all my cousins around. My grandmother would even crack jokes saying that I was the little old lady in the shoe, with all of my husband's kids over from other women, coming by, and I had my own. She said "He needs to stop letting those women just drop off their kids whenever they want to, you are not the babysitter," She would get upset about that. Summer time, I had a house full of kids. . We laughed and listened to music. When it was good it was really good, but, when it was bad it was really bad.

I tried to leave him a few times, but it was like I had no one to turn to that would help me. First reason is nobody really knew how bad it really was, I was not announcing our fights. Most of them were behind closed doors or when our children were not home. I mentioned it to my grandmother a few times. Sad to say the women in her day had the mentality that if a man is taking care of you financially as good as he was taking care of me, you must be doing something wrong to make him act that way. She did not know the details of the abuse, how brutal and life threatening that the fights were. As for the other people who may have known more, such as my cousins, he would bribe them with his money. They were not accustomed to being around real money and they were just easily manipulated. I thought they cared for me but reality is that they did not. I was the cousin that was never around, the one that they did not grow up with. I was the pretty brown skin cousin from California with the "good hair". They even made jokes that me and my sister were the "Pretty Bitches." Our grandmother's favorites". These cousins were on my mom's side of the family. Later one of them turned on me and it could have ended my life!

People can be cold and especially if they are jealous. Jealousy is something that I never want to have. It is dangerous. Everything in that relationship got twisted. As I was saying, one of my cousins whom I had just met on my mother's side of the family had left her abusive alcoholic husband. They had five kids with a father that did not help them financially at all, so I helped her kids - I always had a glow for kids, they were always so innocent and sweet in my eyes, especially compared to everything else in this world.

She and I had begun to hang out a lot and we were getting really close, at least that is what I thought. I tried to help her as much as I could, I arranged for him to let her move into one of our houses so that she could leave her children's father and I told him to paint her kids room the same way that my kids rooms were painted, the girls pink and the boys blue. I bought her oldest son his first pair of named brand Jordan tennis shoes.. I really had love for her and her children. There was nothing I wouldn't do for them. She wound up turning against me, lying on me to him and telling him that I cheated on him, she slept with my husband. I was always around scandalous females that liked the fact that he had a business and money. They would do anything for it including betraying their own family. I realized that you have to be careful of people that have no loyalty and are wolves in sheep's clothing. The last person she should have done anything like this too was me, once again I believed in someone that backstabbed me.

My husband had other kids that weren't mine, and one of them was a 16-year-old boy who tried to protect me from him. He had pretty much started to catch inappropriate feelings for me because I was always around, more than his dad, taking him to sports practice and supporting him at his games and at his high school. I was up at the school making sure he kept his grades up, I was just being a stepmom to him, I treated him as if he was my own child even though he was a little too old to be my own. I cared about him and wanted him to be happy and successful, he didn't want to see me constantly battered emotionally and physically.

One day he told me, you're too beautiful for my dad to treat you like that - hitting you, cheating on you, and making you be friends with girls that he's cheating on you with. I was so shocked because I did not know that he knew what was going on. One night I was up late, pasting the floors, crying and really depressed. I had been calling my husband all day and night and he was not answering my calls. I started calling hotels and motels, I was really losing it. My stepson came into the living room and he said" don't cry over that guy". He said that he loved his dad but he hates the way that his dad treats me. He went on to say that I am too good for him. I said "what are you talking about"? He went on to say," You want me to tell you where he is right now?" He is at Tracy's house." Now that name had rang a bell because that was a different childhood friend that he also started bringing around me. I really liked that girl. Her and her two kids even stayed at my house for a while. I thought she was his cousin. His mother and her mother were best friends. So I was shocked.

Tracy was light skinned with really long pretty hair, she had a big butt also, she was always going through some drama of her own with one of her baby's fathers. I would console her and be there for her. He always admired her hair. He really liked pretty hair, my hair is what they call "good hair" also but Tracy's hair was really long. I was filled with rage when my step son told me that she and my husband were messing around. I needed confirmation. I got the address from my step son to her new place. I went over to her house, looked through the window. Sure enough I saw him sitting on the couch and she leaned over him like she was about to kiss him. I banged on the front door, while looking in the window. He saw me, and did not say a word. I said" I know that you are in there, I see you and her, open up the damn door or I am going to bust out the windows"! He still remained quiet, so I walked over to his new car and slashed the tires. I was furious and tired of him. At that point, I did not care if he was going to beat me up or not.

He had already cheated on me with my family, so-called friends, and beat me up. I was one foot out the door. He came home later that night and he did not do anything at all. He pretended like it never happened. I was confused, but life just went on as usual.

During our years together I wanted to go to school on more than one occasion. I always had the desire to do something in the medical field. I got my CNA (Certified Nursing Assistant) certificate when I was 22 yrs. old, and before that I was a home health care aid. When I first met him, that was one of the trades that I did. I received the Home Health Aide certificate when I was 18 yrs old. I always had a love for the nursing field. I did not like blood so I always wanted to do things that did not require too much blood activity. I figured that if I was to get a nursing license that I could continue working with the elderly people, because I loved it.

One day I surprised him and went to the school and took the pretest in order to see if I qualified for the expedited class that was being offered at that time. I passed the test and filled out my financial aid paperwork and received my books. I was so very excited when I went home I could not wait until he came home so that I could tell him the great news! I heard the car coming into the driveway of our big brick house. I ran outside because I was so excited I could not even wait until he came into the house. I greeted him in the driveway and ran to the driver side window and said : Guess what! I passed the test and I was accepted in the nursing class, look at my books." He looked at my books in my hand along with my pager and notebooks. Grabbed them all from me and threw them on the ground. Then he took his big Land Cruiser truck that he had at the time and ran my books and the pager over. Then he reversed the car and ran them over again a second time. I said :"Why did you do that"? He said because you don't need to go to school right now, all you need to do is take care of these kids and this house. I said I have a baby sitter and school is part time. He said I do not care, you are not going to school right now.

That is when that financial abuse came in. He only wanted me to make the money he wanted me to make and only work for our company, so that he could control the money. I never was able to save on my own. He controlled all of the money. I could have access to the bank and use whatever I needed but he never wanted me to have my own, only ours.

I tried to go to school again a few years later to be a phlebotomist. It was strictly an online class and I did not have to leave the house. Also, the children were a little older now so I thought I would try again. I felt it was perfect timing. I also felt that the extra income in the house would be good.

Seeing that he liked to gamble and sometimes the money would go as fast as it came in, maybe if I also made money I could make sure that we saved for our kids' future. That always meant so much to me. But by this time we had been together for over ten years and he established an addiction to gambling. We did have a successful real estate business as real estate investors and rehabbing neighborhoods. Despite the success we still had financial issues at times due to his gambling. When he won it was great but when he lost it was a big loss and it was not a stable lifestyle to have. I tried to stop him many times but he was out of control.

I was hoping he would be excited about me starting school this time. But once again he said the same thing as before when I wanted to take the nursing class. Why are you going to school? Now is not the time. I realized the time for him was never. Even if my intentions are to get a good career to have part time to help save for the children's college education and other things. It meant nothing. He was a control freak. To lose control of my financial freedom was something that he was not having.

Financial abuse is real and it is not ok. Being a wife and being submissive is great, I do believe in that. I also believe that your wife should be your partner and decisions should be talked over between the two of you. You should love your wife as you love yourself, I am sure that he would not have liked someone controlling and abusing his life in so many different ways.

At one point, despite all our success, he wound up in jail for a misdemeanor for six months, we all ended up staying with his mom. Which was his idea. Maybe so that she could watch us. He would have to stay at the jail at night, get out and work all day, and then go back to jail again that evening. They call it a Work Release Program in Ohio.. One day he came home before going back into the jail. We were all at his mom's house when he came out for a few hours, including his ex-wife, so that he could see his other kids that he had with her. He asked what we were going to eat and I suggested we could have hot dogs because I was tired. I had been dealing with the kids all day. Well, he didn't like that even one bit, so he got up and decided to make a clown with me while I was sitting there with my own kids. He grabbed the mustard and walked up to me and said, "this is what I think about hot dogs, and poured it all over my head. He did the same thing with the ketchup, spraying it over my hair and face, and then again with the relish. I was in shock. His ex-wife kind of laughed at first until she saw how everyone else was acting, and my kids were all crying seeing him acting like this. Eventually his ex-wife said, "Stop doing that to that girl, you are crazy? "She had a taste of his abuse as well. Maybe not as bad as mine, but she definitely had her share.

I am not sure what type of day that he had in jail, all I knew was I was not even thirty years old yet, and I was tired. Tired of living a life like that, tired of him, tired of watching all his kids with no gratitude or appreciation shown to me, tired of being a good wife. Just TIRED!

Finally, one day I decided it was time to get clear of him and I decided to take a trip back to California with my grandmother. She invited me and I was really excited.. She and I both knew that I needed to get away. We planned the trip a couple of weeks in advance. She and her husband could tell that I was having second thoughts about the trip because of my husband. He said I could go first. Then a few days before it was time to go he started saying that he didn't want me to go. The only reason he said I could go in the first place is because my Grandmother asked, not me. It was hard for him to say no to my Grandmother, he did not want to look like the bad guy. So we had prepared to go and I was taking my oldest daughter with me. She was not going to stay home and help him babysit the other kids. We had been preparing for weeks. The day before leaving I called and told my grandmother I was not going. She said oh yes you are! I already bought these tickets and you are going. So I went to sleep.

I heard a knock on the door early in the morning around 5:00 am. It was my Grandmother and her husband, they came to my house to get me. When he told my grandmother that he didn't think it was a good idea, she cut him off while he was talking, right in the middle of his sentence, saying " I already bought the tickets, she is going." Then she looked over at me and said, "Now go and get your things together." Because by this point my

Grandmother knew that I was very unhappy and tired, she said I needed a break.

He went upstairs to take a shower and I was packing for my trip when his phone started ringing. I answered it and it was one of my female cousins and she asked to speak to him. I asked her why in the world she would need to talk to him and she just started laughing and said "he knows what I need to talk to him about". I was appalled, embarrassed, and humiliated all at once. I demanded that he tell me what was going on, and what they needed to talk about as soon as he got out of the shower. Instead he got out of the shower and grabbed my leg and twisted it as hard as he could. Pain went screaming through me, I said underneath my breath in a low tone, "Yea, that's ok, that's why I am leaving you," Maybe for that reason, I finally got up the nerve to get in the car with my grandmother and get out of Ohio. I was tired. I did not care anymore nor did I love him anymore. As a matter of fact not only did I not love him anymore, I could not stand him.

We went to the train station and he kept calling me and harassing me saying, "You know we have a real estate deal that we need to close on. "He was trying to manipulate me to stay, baby, I am gone, it felt so good to go!

CHAPTER 7

I'M GOING BACK TO CALI

When I got to California, I never wanted to go back home. I didn't care about anything. Not money, not property, nothing. My oldest daughter was with me and we were finally free. I felt like I had just been released from prison. I have never been to prison, but I felt as if I could feel what it would be like. I remember sitting in my sister's backyard not doing anything in particular but watching the sun rise and feeling the breeze on my face and realizing for the first time in forever, I didn't have to worry about what someone else was plotting against me. I did not have to look over my shoulder. I did not have to walk on eggshells anymore. I didn't have to worry about what was going on behind my back and I did not have to be afraid of saying or doing the wrong thing. It was a kind of peace like nothing I had ever felt before, I could really hear the birds chirping and the warm air felt so good, with the sun shining on my face, I still can imagine that feeling because it was a feeling I never felt before, as if I came from drowning in water to land, it felt like a breath of fresh air, at that moment I realized God's plan for me was not to be in this terrible situation and always feeling physical, emotional and mental pain.

I was really enjoying being in California, I felt like I was back at home again. It was a beautiful hot summer and it felt so good to be home. I was driving around with my mom and sister, getting our nails done and I felt beautiful again. It felt like the good ole days, even better. It took me back to when I was a child before my cycles of abuse started. When life feels good, the air feels good, and I can feel the peace in the air. I felt as if I could really have a future of peace. In my mind I knew that feeling this way is how my life should be and I had no plans on going back to my life of hurt.

My daughter had a beautiful voice and she could sing. Everyone loved to hear her sing. She was singing at the Bar-B-Ques that we were invited to. It felt like we could really have a real life and be ok here in California. Even my daughter seemed more at peace. I know that my life of pain was also affecting her. I was always drifting into a daydream and just thanking God for the moment and in awe and disbelief that I was in California without him, I really had it made up in my mind that I never wanted to go back. I forgot what it felt like to live.

One day my brother had made plans for us to go out to dinner and after dinner we went to the beach, as it was starting to get dark as the sun was going down.. Along with me and my brother he had a friend come along. His friend was a really nice person, he had a sincere soul, he treated me like a queen. I was not accustomed to being handled gently and admired. We had really good communication. We went to the beach and started hanging out a lot. It was nothing sexual, just spending a lot of time together, a genuine connection. It was such a natural feeling with that guy because of how sweet he was treating me. We both loved the beach. One day we went to the beach together and I will always remember this day. He walked me out in the water, as the waves were coming, we walked out into the sun, he looked into my eyes and told me how beautiful I was, he kissed me so gently. I had not felt like that in a long time, maybe never. All I know is I felt love for him because of the way that he treated me. He felt love for me also, but it didn't work out because he wanted me to be totally over my ex and he felt like he was just a rebound. Maybe he was a rebound, but it felt good to be treated like a lady, and I knew that I was over my ex. Those feelings had been left. I may have fallen in love with that feeling after being abused for so many years.

My ex and I were still married and had kids together. I didn't want to go back to Ohio ever, but I couldn't just leave things the way they were, either. My husband found out about me and the guy from California because my sister told him when he called, thinking that would make him stop harassing her because he was calling every few minutes asking where I was. My sister was persistent in saying that I should go back to Ohio to get money from my husband. She said to me "How are you going to make it out here, California is expensive, just go back and see if he will give you some money to help you out. At the same time, he was insisting that he had forgiven me for meeting someone new and wanted to give me money, so I would not have to struggle in California. He had a way of manipulating anyone to believe his lies. My sister had spoken to him one day when I was not at home and he manipulated her as well and she actually did believe him. I knew him very well, so I was so wary of going back to Ohio because I was afraid of him, I do not think my sister really realized how crazy he was, he promised not to put his hands on me and he even told people in my family that he would not hurt me, he bribed me by saying that he needed me to come home and close a deal that would net us a profit of $60,000, and he would split it 50-50 with me. I didn't have any money in California because he had closed my access to all the accounts when I left Ohio.

I had the pressure of other people telling me that going back to Ohio was the best thing to do. It is amazing to me how my loved ones were trying to persuade me to go back to a man that beat on me. The cycle of abuse that was obviously around me at the time was sad. It was a time in my life that lots of people in my circle were struggling and it felt like the only thing that mattered to everyone was money. I was caught on the web. I remember feeling like if I did not go back to him I would no longer have a place to stay in California because I did not have enough money without getting more from him. So, I went back to Ohio against my better judgment.

CHAPTER 8

GUT INSTINCT

When I first arrived he was being cool. He seemed happy to see me. He picked me up from the airport with my child in the car. We went to eat and then to our house. I was excited to see my kids and they were happy to see me as well. It appeared as if everything was going good and going in the direction as he and I had discussed. But inside of my gut I was still feeling uneasy. Once I got there, he kept pushing the closing date of the escrow of the house back more and more to get me to stay longer. I had already been there for a couple of weeks and I was ready to go. He was trying to make me feel like he was changing as a person and that he had broken his cycle of abuse with me. He also came from a background of abuse because his dad also abused his mom when they were together. Even though he appeared to have changed, I was not falling for it. See, as a Rnb singer said a while ago, there isn't anything that you can do about it when a woman is fed up. Maybe time and patience could mend things but at that moment I was done and just wanted to go back to my "paradise land" of California.

So, after trying hard to deal with being back in Ohio and dealing with facing the man that I no longer want to be with or have any feelings for. Trying to hold it all together so that I do not push his buttons either. I knew that in the back of his mind he knew that I wanted to leave him and he also knew that I was dealing with another man while in California. I know this man very well, and I know that he is a ticking time bomb ready to explode. I was walking on eggshells, every day.

Until one day, I had enough. It was time for me to speak up. I was more and more nervous every day being there. I was very scared of him and I really just wanted to leave. This led me to speak up one day as I was lying in bed, I told him, "Look, I am tired of waiting, I will sign my part of the profit over to you, you told me that it would just take a few days and that you will support my move to California, I just want to go back to California!" Nobody else was home but me, him, and my two-year-old baby son. When I said I wanted to leave, my then husband completely lost control of himself. He got angry and had a crazy look on his face, he said ok, and started to beat me so hard in my body that I could barely walk when it was over. He was punching me with a closed fist in my ribs and stomach, arms and everywhere, he even hit me in my face this time. He started choking me and the veins were popping out of my neck, I felt like

I was going to die right then and there. My son was saying "Daddy, stop doing that, you're hurting Mommy." as my child was starting to cry, his father was having a psychotic moment. He had the nerve to tell my son that we were just playing and being silly, and then he went right back to beating on me. As I was starting to lose my breath and hope, I was praying to God inside saying, "Get me out of this, I'll never come back, I won't worry about the money." and in that brief moment I looked at my husband, and I couldn't see his face, instead I saw something that looked like a Beast, with horns and dark brown skin. I closed my eyes and opened them again and saw the same thing and realized that this man was transformed into a devil. Some type of spirit must have gotten into him, I knew that I had to get free of him. This is not an example; this is a fact I literally saw that image. I have never seen it since then.

I tried to gouge out his eyeballs but that just made him angrier and he released me for a minute as I tried to run. He grabbed me and grabbed a pillow like he was going to smother me. At that moment, God took over me and guided me with his spirit and I started saying anything I could to get him to stop, telling him I loved him and I didn't want to leave him, that I was just scared and I wanted to stay with him forever, I really do not remember everything that I was saying at that moment because the holy spirit took over my words. Whatever I said that night, worked. At first he didn't believe me, but I kept talking to him until he did and he released me and started hugging me, even as I was still coughing and choking and crying.

He had told me to get in our jacuzzi bath tub and then he disappeared to the basement and came back with a gun. I asked him if he was going to kill me and he said that he felt like he should kill himself because he had beaten me again after promising he wouldn't. But it was all just an act on his part. He had no remorse about what he was doing. He was completely unhinged by then. To this day I believe that he pretended like he was going to take his own life because he knew that he promised not to hit me again. He felt like that was a way for me to feel sorry for him. He also thought the neighbors might have heard me screaming so he whispered and said "come on let's go, the neighbors may have heard you." I did not get up right away because I was still very scared, hoping that the neighbors did hear me and that the police would come and rescue me from the house of hell. He had a gun and he was saying let's go! He said "The neighbors may have heard us and heard you screaming", let's go to the hotel. I was petrified and traumatized at this point. I got up and said ok.

As I was shaking, I gathered our things, the clothes on our backs and a few things for the baby and took my son and spent the night at a hotel in case the neighbors called the cops. I did not even pack any clothes or jewelry, we just rushed out of the house.

All I could think is what is next. I prayed to God and eventually fell asleep.

The next morning, we woke up, threw on the same clothes and went to breakfast. Afterwards, he took me to the mall and spent a lot of money on me. It wasn't to be nice though, it was to hide all the damage physically and in hopes that I would feel better inside, he wanted to cover up what he had done to me the night before. He bought me these giant name brand expensive sunglasses to cover up my black eyes, gold jewelry to hide the broken capillaries on my neck, a new gold bracelet and new clothes to cover up my bruises. Sad to say, he had plenty of practice in knowing what to buy to cover up his dirty work. He also did that to make up for hurting me.

After changing clothes, we went to my oldest son's football game, while other parents tried to talk to me, smiling and discussing the game. I was just in a daze, trying to figure out how I was going to get out of this terrible mess. I just remember literally ignoring them as they spoke to me. My body was in agony and I had to sit there and pretend everything was nice and normal. All I was thinking is, why did I come back to this place? Why didnt I listen to my gut instinct? Am I going to get out of here alive this time? Will he start thinking about the new friend I met in California and try to kill me again? With all of these thoughts racing through my head all I wanted to do was leave, and by all means necessary I knew that is what I had to do. I had grown to hate him. I despised him; he was not even attractive to me anymore. His horrible ways had finally gotten me to the point that I was done!

My football playing son was about twelve at the time, he spent the night at a friend's house that night of the fight, he had no idea of what had happened, and after the game, my two sons, my husband at the time and I stopped at a gas station so he could run in and get a drink. For whatever reason, that's the moment where I decided it was time to get the hell away from him once and for all. While he was inside, I just drove off and left him at the gas station. Yes, I really just drove off and left him in the store. I had never done anything like that before. I know that he was in shock because I even shocked myself. I was really in survival mode at that moment. I remember praying to God to please let me be safe and free as I drove away.

The next 24 hours were some of the most uncertain and defining times of my entire life. I kept trying to reach out for help and couldn't seem to find it anywhere. I drove to his mother's house first because she was watching my daughters during the game, but he had already beat me to it and he called her and told his mother that I wasn't allowed to take any of his kids because he knew I was trying to leave Ohio. That was true for the daughters that we shared, but my oldest daughter was only mine, and so I made my mother-in-law have her come downstairs and she came down to join us.

I phoned my father and asked if I could come by, I told him that I was in a fight with my husband, he said yes and I went to my father's house next. By the time I arrived I saw him outside with his girlfriend at the time. He walked over to my car and leaned over the window and started talking to me. He told me that he had just got off the phone with my husband, and he was on his way over to smooth things out because we had only had a little argument. I flipped out when I heard this. "Little argument, I said ", I took off my glasses so that he could see that my eye was black, then I showed him my neck, you could see red broken vessels in my neck, I showed my dad all of my bruises. He was in shock, he apologized to me for telling my husband that I was on the way there to his house and then he said that I should report it to the police. I told my dad that I needed to leave before he came and found me. I drove off and left my father's house, trying to make sure that I did not run into my husband.

Me and my kids drove to the police station next and were told that there was no room for us at any of the battered women's shelters in the area. I was flabbergasted by this. At long last, after all these years of abuse I go to the police and they shoot me down. I asked if one of them could escort me to my house to get clothes for myself and the kids, and they said they could only do that if I filed a police report against my then husband. Stupidly, I refused to do so because he had a felony conviction in the past, when he was eighteen, he only got probation then and I knew if I got him arrested, he'd be in jail for good and my kids would never see their dad again. Or at least not for a long time. I did not want that to happen. All I wanted was to be free from him and safe.

I felt like I was quickly running out of options, so I called a friend and stayed at her house overnight with my kids. I knew I wanted to leave the state, I just needed time to think of a plan. It felt good staying at my friend Tiffany's house because I did feel safe there. She was also very funny and just a cool person to be around. She was like family. She gave us something to eat, although I did not have much of an appetite. After dinner, she and I were talking and it felt really good to vent to someone and not feel judged. Although she said that I could stay as long as I wanted to, I called my mom and told her what was going on and she agreed to get help from my sister's boyfriend to send me some money to help me to get back to California. I knew that I could never really feel safe in Ohio with my husband living there, everyone that I knew also knew him, I did not feel safe and it felt like for me to ever move on, break the cycle and start a new life without looking over my shoulders, I would have to leave Ohio. So that is exactly what I did.

I put my children back in the SUV and I drove to the western end of Ohio. When stopping to get gas I noticed that he had turned off the only credit card that I had on me, he must've reported it stolen. I called my mom back to see if she was able to borrow the money. My mom had someone to Western Union deliver the money that she had come up with for me to get to California. It was a Godsend because all I had were the clothes on my back and those on the back of my kids. I drove us all the way from Cleveland back to California, about 2,500 miles, to finally get free of this man that I can't believe I once thought that I loved.

CHAPTER 9

FEAR OF THE UNKNOWN

While being free of him was a blessing that I have never stopped thanking God for, fear of the unknown was always one of the reasons that I was afraid to take bold steps and leave. Well now I was literally living in the unknown and I had to give it my very best. Nobody said life was easy and starting over sure was not easy. Living in California still started off as a struggle. It was a challenge finding a place to live with little money and I was even homeless a few times as I tried to get back on my feet. I had to sleep in hotels and in my car. I didn't really believe in being on welfare or public assistance because I came from a background of people that worked, My mom worked and her mom worked. I also remember my grandmother always saying that she does not respect women that just have babies to get welfare and those types of women are lazy, all of those things stuck and played over and over in my cluttered brain. Then I started remembering a conversation that me and my grandmother also had. She said I am not totally against welfare or public assistance. However, she went on to say that welfare/public assistance is supposed to be a stepping stone for people to get on their feet, it is not a permanent form of income. So that is exactly what I used it for. There are programs that will help women in Domestic violence situations to get a babysitter and to get public assistance so that they can get on their feet. I chose to do it, it was a humbling decision, and while I was getting food stamps and money, I was looking for a job. God is definitely good, I started working shortly after I was on public assistance. I walked into a Home Health Care Agency in Ontario, California. I had an interview with two beautiful black women. I was so impressed because they owned the Health Care Agency. Although I did not have much experience in that field, they gave me a shot and hired me to be the head of Human Resources. I could not believe I was an HR administrator overseeing several other people for the company. She was a good person, a black woman that owned her own business, who decided to take a chance on me. I started to realize that there are still good people in the world.

I got a place for us to live in Ontario, California, and we started really doing some living again. Of course, my ex wouldn't leave me alone. He called me a lot. He threatened me that if I didn't bring his youngest son back, he would kill me. I made sure

I was never in his presence again for a while, having my brother meet him to give him his son back at a halfway point. I just wanted to get a divorce and be done with him, and that naivete cost me a lot of things. I was broke while he still had our business, so he hired a good attorney and made sure everything went his way in the divorce. He asked me how I would want to split up the kids, because that was my option. That was a very hard decision to make so I suggested that he keep the boys and I have custody of the girls in the divorce because that would be the easiest, but he refused that and said he wanted one of the girls, he chose the daughter that he wanted. He only did that to make things more stressful for me and to hurt me. He wanted to make sure that he had something that I wanted, which of course the kids.

When the divorce papers came I signed off on them, even though it meant no money, no alimony, no child support, nothing, not even all the girls. He had residential custody of his chosen kids and I had residential custody of mines that he also chose. Which also meant nobody pays anybody any child support. All I got out of it was my freedom, but I think back to that night I saw him in his true form when he almost killed me, and that's all I was asking God for, to let me survive that night and get free of him, and that's exactly what God delivered.

Even then, it was a struggle to get free of him. When my kids would go to visit him from California to Ohio, he would try to keep them there by bribing them, telling them he had so much money he could buy them whatever they wanted. They would get on the phone and tell me, "Mommy I want to stay here with daddy because he said that I can do gymnastics if I am here with him and if I go with you, I cannot do nothing." It hurt so bad to hear them say those types of things to me. In my mind I knew that he was more financially together than me because I was trying to get on my feet from having nothing. You would think that he would just pay for them to join the sports while with me, which is what a father that genuinely loves their children and wants the best for the child would do. Not him, he did not want them to be happy with me, see, it wasn't about the kid's happiness it was more about hurting me. I started to realize his manipulative game. The children did not understand the game and I looked like the bad guy plenty of times to them. He put me through so much heartache, headaches, and tears, even from a distance. It felt like he was trying to get them to like him more than me. I knew that I had to let all of that go. I had to let go of giving him the time over the phone to hurt me and let go of even seeing my kids as much as I wanted to because he was making everything so hard for me. I knew that I had to concentrate on getting myself together and stop giving him my energy. There's a time and place for everything and I knew that at that time I needed to concentrate on my main player, which was myself.

The further I got away from him mentally and released him from my brain the better things went for me. I've sold cars for a living for a short time, got a job in human resources, then I became a loan officer for a mortgage company, account executive for a bank, and a property manager. I became a licensed realtor in both California and Georgia also working as a project manager for investors by rehabbing their homes and making them turn key ready to either sell or rent out. I got back to making good money again. I am a jack of all trades through this journey. I needed to find myself and get to know myself again and figure out what I truly wanted from myself as well as from life and others.

I will be honest when I tell you that I had a couple of other bad relationships after my break-up and divorce. Not as abusive, but not good either. But that's a little like saying that I got shot in the leg instead of getting shot in the chest. Either way, it's a terrible situation that never should have happened. It was a journey and a marathon. I had to realize that getting things back comfortable took time. I learned how not to be so hard on myself when I was not where I wanted to be in life. I had to start over at the age of thirty when most people are just getting to where they wanted to be. I had to realize that my life is different and not to be compared to others.

I had to do some soul searching, I have read plenty of self-help books, self-healing books and the bible. I have prayed so much. God is probably like, what does my problem child want now (haha). I have made a trillion mistakes and I feel like those events needed to happen so that I can help others. I know that some people are probably thinking, why would I want to tell all my dirty laundry? Truthfully, as I was writing this book I was thinking, wow girl, you really went through it, are you really ready to share all of this and open up your life to the public, to possibly get judged? Believe it or not, I am a very private person, which gives me all the reason to believe that this is simply my purpose. When I started gaining momentum and hitting my stride, that's when I realized that I needed to be giving back to other women facing the same circumstances that I went through. That's what my nonprofit organization, New Life Choice, is all about. I want to touch the lives of other women and let them see all the things I went through in hopes that they can avoid having the same thing happen to them. New Life Choice is the name of the organization because YOU HAVE A CHOICE OF A NEW LIFE. A life that you deserve. As you saw from the statistics at the front of this book, a huge chunk of women who go through what I did end up unemployed, battered, psychologically damaged, addicted to drugs, or dead. That's not hyperbole and it's not meant to scare you, it's the cold hard facts of the matter. At the time that I left my ex-husband we were getting a house built from the ground up, my dream home. We were successful in business and had lots of grown-up toys, such as jet skis, nice cars, fancy clothes, jewelry and real estate. I left all of that behind for peace of mind and safety. I chose to have a new life. I would leave him again If I had to replay it. I do not regret leaving him. I just wish I would have left sooner. Words cannot describe how it felt after leaving him. It is like being in the matrix and realizing for the first time that you were in the matrix. I got so accustomed to being treated the wrong way that once I realized I was free it didn't feel real. I was able to live again. Life is not long and tomorrow is not promised. I deserve to be happy and so do you, beloved.

I learned that my past does not define who I am. I am not my past. If you let the things that you have been through rule your life by dwelling on them or becoming a bitter woman, you will be cheating yourself of what you truly deserve. Until you can let it go and learn to love again, you will only be hurting yourself and robbing yourself of life. I am now a Real Estate Agent, licensed in two states. I have closed many deals and I also have rehabbed homes and sold them for profit, by myself. I managed my oldest daughter's career as a singer and songwriter and she was signed to Universal publishing. My children are doing well and are business owners, some are homeowners and none are on drugs or anything too bad. We have our ups and downs, no, life is not perfect, but it is great and I am so blessed. I am one of the ones who seeped through the cracks, but I know that most women in the situation I was in, where it got so violent so frequently ended up dead. But I'm here to tell you that you don't have to keep living in that nightmare. At the end of the road, at the end of the rainbow, there is a pot of gold that is you having your own life back. Your freedom back. Living life to the fullest.

You might be at the point where you want to get out of an abusive relationship but you don't know how. I'm going to tell you the way that worked for me and that I know can work for you.

The first step is to get down on your knees and pray for direction from God. Whether you've been in church every Sunday for the past 40 years or you only talk to God when you're trying to pick your lottery numbers, this is the time to trust in him and give all of your worries, and fears, and doubts over to him, trusting him to take care of you and to guide you in the steps that are going to get you free. It might not happen right away, but you need to listen to His voice, not the one telling you to stay with this man, no matter how many times he tells you that he will change or it's going to be different or any other lines and lies he feeds you to try and keep you from leaving. He will not change. Unless he truly wants to find God and get professional help. Abuse is a sickness.

The next step is to have a serious support system in place. I did not have one and it cost me dearly, both in time and in the violence and suffering that my children and I endured until I finally got into a situation where we could break free for good. No one in my circle seemed to think that what my ex was doing was all that bad, but of course I also didn't share all the details with them. My grandmother thought I should stay with a man if he was giving me money and taking care of me. Two of my cousins who I thought would have my back ended up sleeping with my husband. I couldn't rely on my mom, either at that time. My dad refused to acknowledge how bad the situation was until I stood in front of him and showed him my bruises and black eyes. If you go to someone and they won't believe you or say they can't help you, keep moving on until you find the right person that does believe you. Make sure you use all the resources at your disposal. Get online, reach out for help, there are more and more facilities out there now helping battered women than there have ever been at any other point in history.

As you move towards getting yourself free, remember to move carefully because this is your life, and if someone who says they love you has no problem hitting you and beating you in good times, it's not difficult to imagine what they might do to you if they find out you're trying to leave them.

When you do get away, cut the ties as much as possible and concentrate on your safety and getting yourself together. Make a point to never be alone anywhere with that person ever again. Always have a friend or a family member with you. It's remarkable how much less brave a domestic abuser is when someone else is around. Remember most abusers are really cowards, that will beat a woman but not so quick to beat a man. So have people near that will be with you so that you can feel safe, at least for a while until things cool off.

Above all else, learn to love yourself. That person who's abusing you does not love you, no matter how much they try to make amends, try to buy your love, and try to tell you that it will never happen again. Those are lies, and you're better than that. You are a strong, powerful, God-fearing woman, and you deserve to be happy and free. You can do this. I believe in you.

As you are making up your mind to break the cycle of abuse and choose a new life for yourself, you will need encouragement. I have found a few scriptures that have helped me to navigate through life. It helps to know that you are not alone. The power of the most high God is real and he will protect you my beloved friend. I wanted to share a few of them with you.

Psalm Chapter 23

A Psalm by David.

Yahweh is my Roeh.
I am never in need.

He makes me lie down in green pastures.
He leads me beside peaceful waters.

He renews my soul.
He guides me along the paths of righteousness
for the sake of his name.

Even though I walk through the dark valley of death,
because you are with me, I fear no harm.
Your rod and your staff give me courage.

You prepare a banquet for me while my enemies watch.
You anoint my head with oil.
My cup overflows.

Certainly, goodness and mercy will stay close to me all the days of my life, and I will remain in Yahweh's house for days without end.

Psalm Chapter 91

Whoever lives under the shelter of Elyon
will remain in the shadow of Shadday.

I will say to Yahweh,
"You are my Machseh and my Metsuda, my Elohim in whom I trust."

He is the one who will rescue you from hunters' traps
and from deadly plagues.

He will cover you with his feathers,
and under his wings you will find refuge.
His truth is your shield and armor.

You do not need to fear
terrors of the night,
arrows that fly during the day,

plagues that roam the dark,
epidemics that strike at noon.

They will not come near you,
even though a thousand may fall dead beside you
or ten thousand at your right side.

You only have to look with your eyes
to see the punishment of wicked people.

You, O Yahweh, are my Machseh!

You have made Elyon your home.

No harm will come to you.
No sickness will come near your house.

He will put his angels in charge of you
to protect you in all your ways.

They will carry you in their hands
so that you never hit your foot against a rock.

You will step on lions and cobras.
You will trample young lions and snakes.

Because you love me, I will rescue you.
I will protect you because you know my name.

When you call me, I will answer you.
I will be with you when you are in trouble.
I will save you and honor you.

I will satisfy you with a long life.
I will show you how I will save you.

Philippians 4:13

I can do everything through Christ who strengthens me.

CHAPTER 10

FORGIVING AND MOVING FORWARD

You have escaped! I am so proud of you! I love you; God loves you and your kids need you. So now it is time to look at yourself as a "Survivor" You are no longer a victim. You are a woman or man of courage and strength. You are a forgiving person and a godly person. A strong and beautiful queen or King. You did it! That is how I feel about myself; I also feel like that about anyone who has left an abusive relationship, male or female. I also feel this way about anyone who has broken any cycles of any form of abuse. You deserve to be happy; you deserve to pat yourself on the back! Celebrate your triumph! So, what do you do now? Well first you remember every morning when you wake up say:" Thank you, thank you, Thank you." This is called "gratitude". Next you will pray. You will pray for strength to make it through the day, you will pray for protection for you and your family and you will pray to forgive. To forgive yourself for your role in this and to forgive the person that hurt you. Then you will go to the mirror and look yourself in the eyes and you will say "I love you "and say your name. As you look in the mirror and say "I love you (your name). And then say: "(Your name) you are so beautiful and so smart and so courageous." Just look at yourself and compliment yourself. It will begin to feel so good. You may even get emotional or shed a tear at first, when you first start this lesson. But as time goes on and you do these things daily you are going to turn into a real "Winner". The magnificent woman or man that you were meant to be. Which is why you are also one those who seeped through the cracks, like me. If you are reading this book and you are going through any form of abuse, just know that you are not alone and you are so special and chosen for another path and purpose. Which is why you are reading this book right now and God has chosen you to still be alive unlike some of the less fortunate women or men that are no longer here with us to read this book or see another day. Some are dead or in jail for killing their abuser. This is the cold and harsh reality of this situation.

Just continue to do these lessons as you are preparing to start your new job and finding your new home. Start loving yourself, taking care of your health and even include a daily workout routine. All of these things will assist in your transition to your new life. As the days go on things will get better. It is a process and in time you will start to see things more clearly. It is a marathon as Nipsey Hussle the Great has quoted, not a sprint.

Even if you may have to struggle for a little while like I did, just remember peace of mind, and your safety is better than where you came from and it is all worth the struggle. Keep a positive attitude, the grass is greener now and the cup is half full not half empty.

If you are reading this book and you are not going through a situation like this, please be sure to pass this book along to someone else that may need to read it. Even if you can save one life it is better than none. I pray that this book will touch the life of a woman or man. I hope that they will see that all that glitters is not gold and that no man, no money, no lifestyle is more important than the gift of life. Your body is your temple. It is precious, not to be abused or taken advantage of. Get your self-esteem back, remember that you are made in the image of God, if you are anything like God you have to be great, the holy spirit is inside of you, which means the spirit of God is inside of you, meaning everything that you need to get away from the abuser is right there inside of you. The strength you need to leave and to make it and make a better life for yourself is inside of you.

I hope that young women and men can pick up something from this book, a "take away", maybe they will be able to pick up on the red flags of a toxic relationship and see that once you are deep in it, there will continue to be a cycle that only gets worse.

The only person that can break the cycle is you, with the strength from within the power of God has your back and your front. I pray that it will help someone to transition from being a victim to becoming a survivor.

DEDICATION

This book is dedicated to my children. Through all that you all have been through, you still manage to make me laugh, smile, cry and I am so very proud of all of you. You always bring me joy.

I also want to dedicate this book to everyone that helped me through this process, sent me the money so that I could drive across the country back to California. You helped in saving my life.

In loving memory of my Grandmother Elma who tried her best to be there for me, I love and appreciate you. I love you.

In loving memory of my heart, My grandmother Susan. She called me "Girlfriend". She said I was like her friend and granddaughter. We became so close and I am so glad you made me take that trip to California with you. "Gone but never forgotten" RIP

I dedicate this to my number 1 and only GOD Yahweh. Without you I would not have been able to tell this story. I also Thank with honor and respect to my mother and my father. Thank you for the love you have given me and the mistakes that you made to allow me to become a better and experienced woman. I genuinely love you both always and forever. A special thanks to my Fiance who I love dearly and who has inspired me to write this book that I am writing now. Be on the lookout for more books - After the cycle is broken. Thank you all, Agape Love

Made in the USA
Monee, IL
09 October 2024